ISSN 2766-4759

Amanda Church

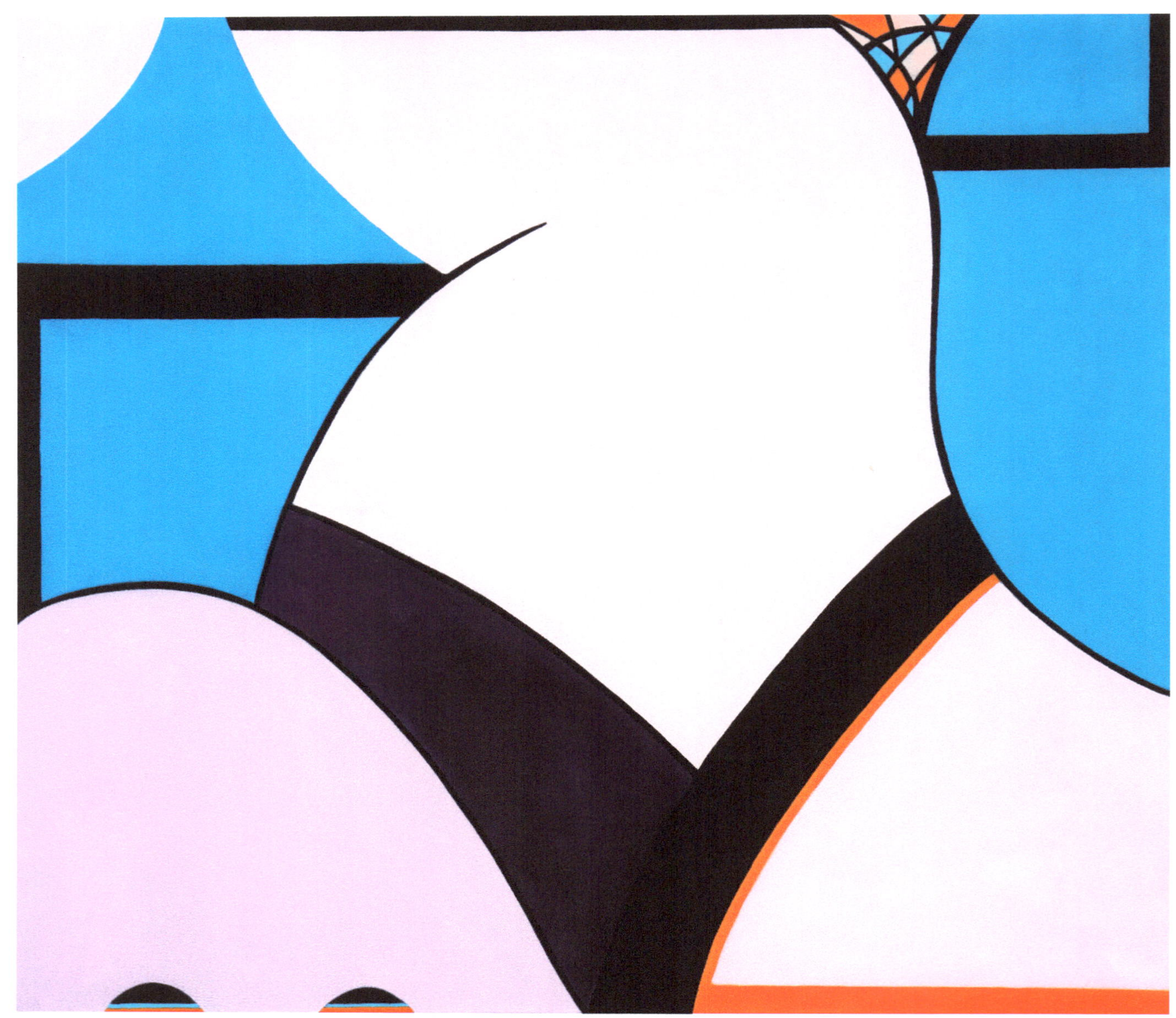

Split 2019 oil on canvas 32 x 36 in.

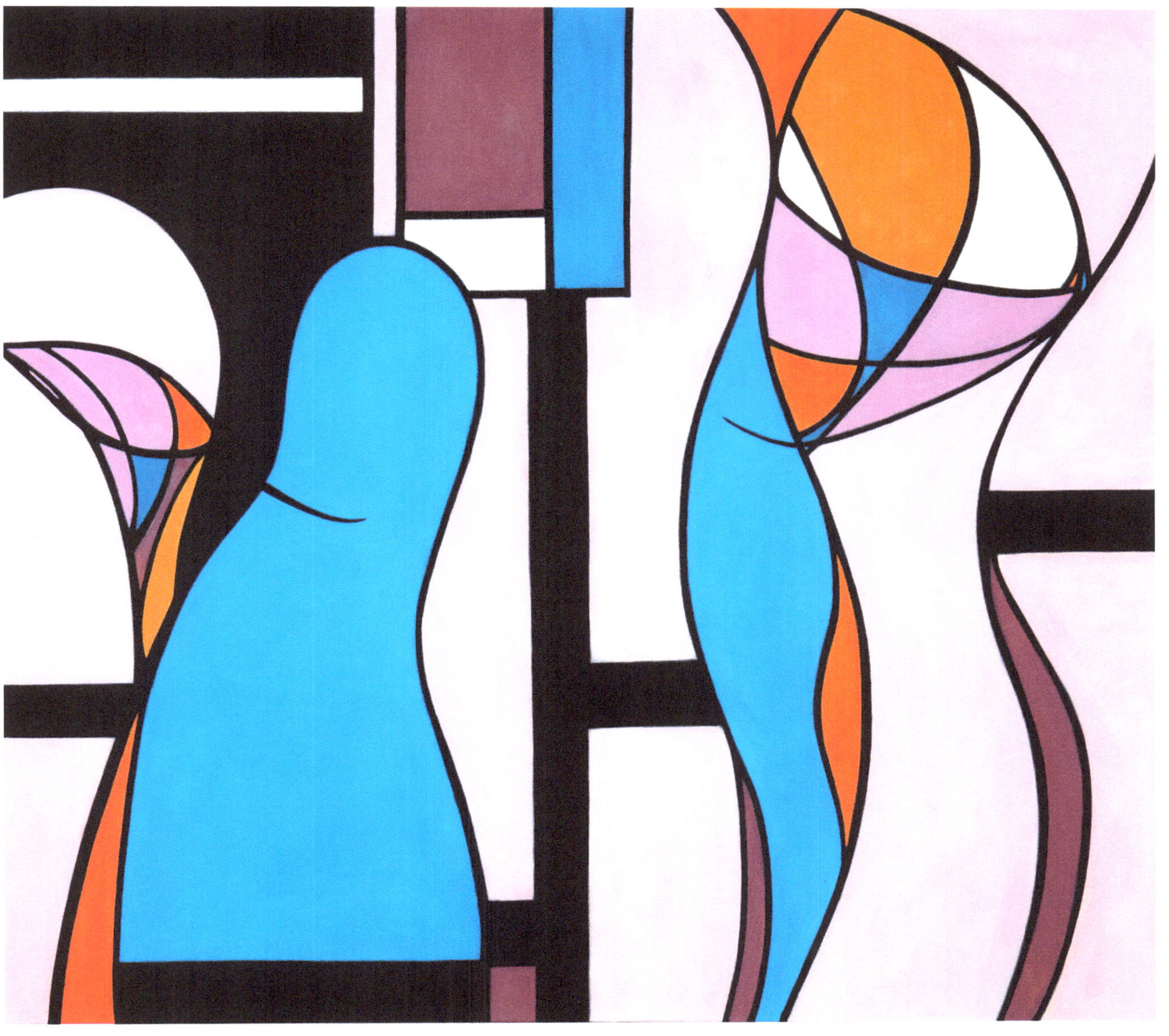

Voyeurs 2019 oil on canvas 32 x 36 in.

Linda Griggs

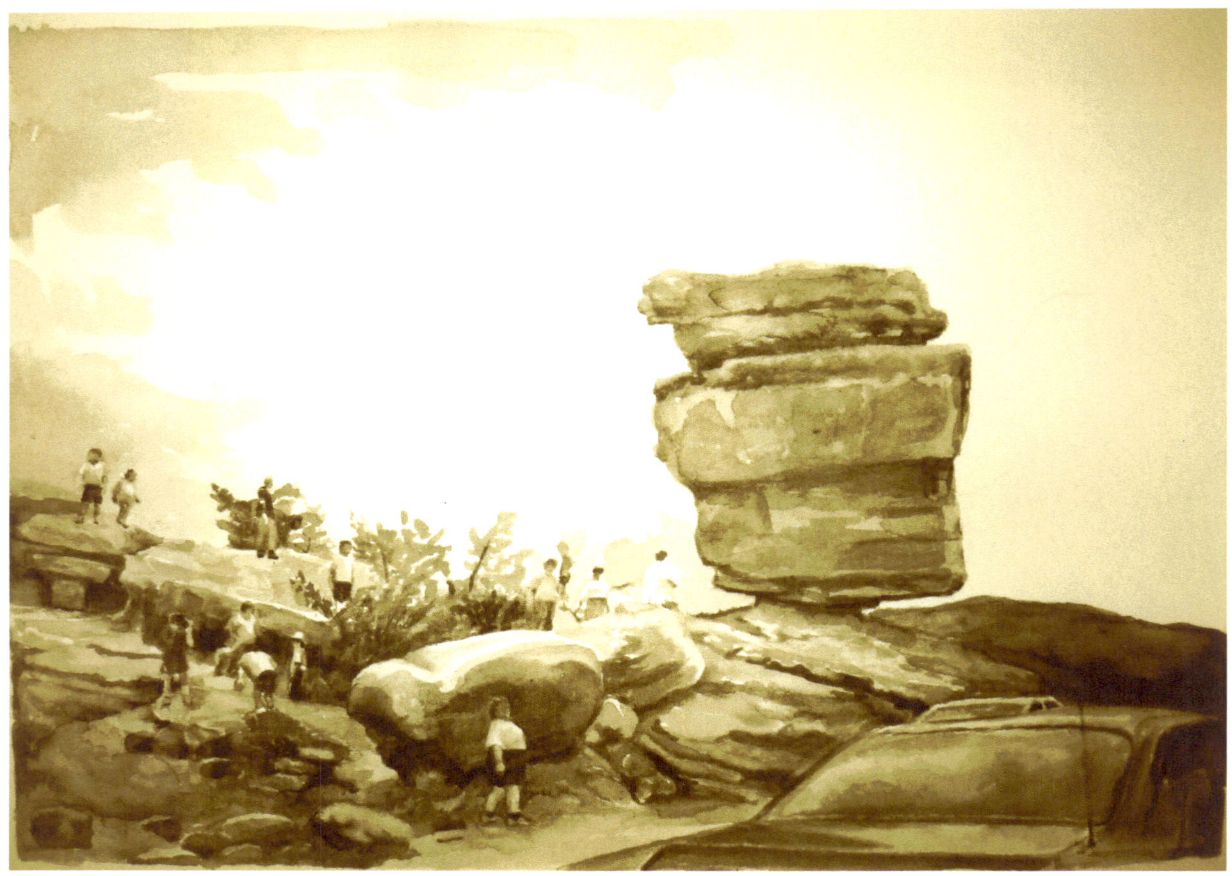

Garden of the Gods 2020 black walnut ink on rives bfk 9¾ x 12½ in.

The Co*v*id Issue

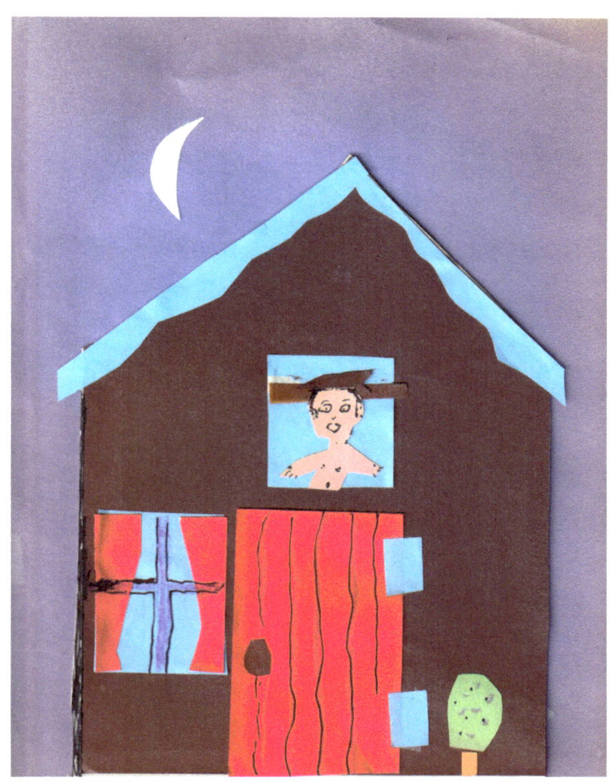

Mordecai's House 2020
Jeffrey Cyphers Wright
Cut paper collage, ink

Publisher and Editor: Jeffrey Cyphers Wright
Deputy Editor: Ilka Scobie
Associate Editor: Lori Ortiz

©2021 Live Mag!
Box 1215 Cooper Sta. NY NY 10276
livemagnyc@gmail.com

https://livemag.org
SUBSCRIBE!

Cover art: JCW; Design: LO

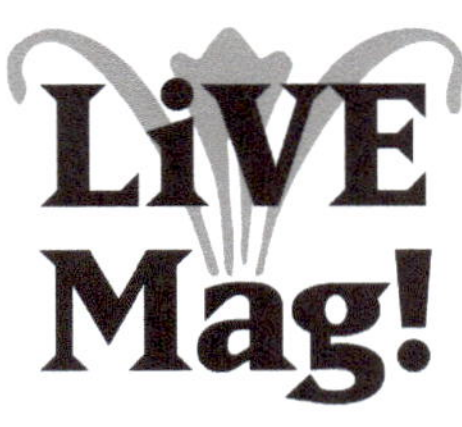

Bob Holman

AWAITING THE RETURN OF THE DRUNK WITH A BROOM

In time, the light of passion returned to his eyes,
And then, suddenly, it was genius or burst!
He'd been dogged by self-mistrust, earnest & true,
What's the matter with you?
Now visions
Stayed put, he could look & talk at the
Same time, he could see through & through it.
His anger at the fools who looked first
At the signature, then at the work — he'd show
'Em! He began sweeping with a vengeance.
It all came back, so very clear, rushing
Towards him! He turned his back as the wave
Broke over him, & swept him out to sea.
Draw this, he said. Draw this poem, I ordered.

What a drama! Harder than walking on water even,
It was more loved than lovely, something you
Can only write down, never endure. Oh,
She uttered, as he rolled over her, fuck me now!
People actually talk like this.
He was inside the painting at the time.

Marina Adams

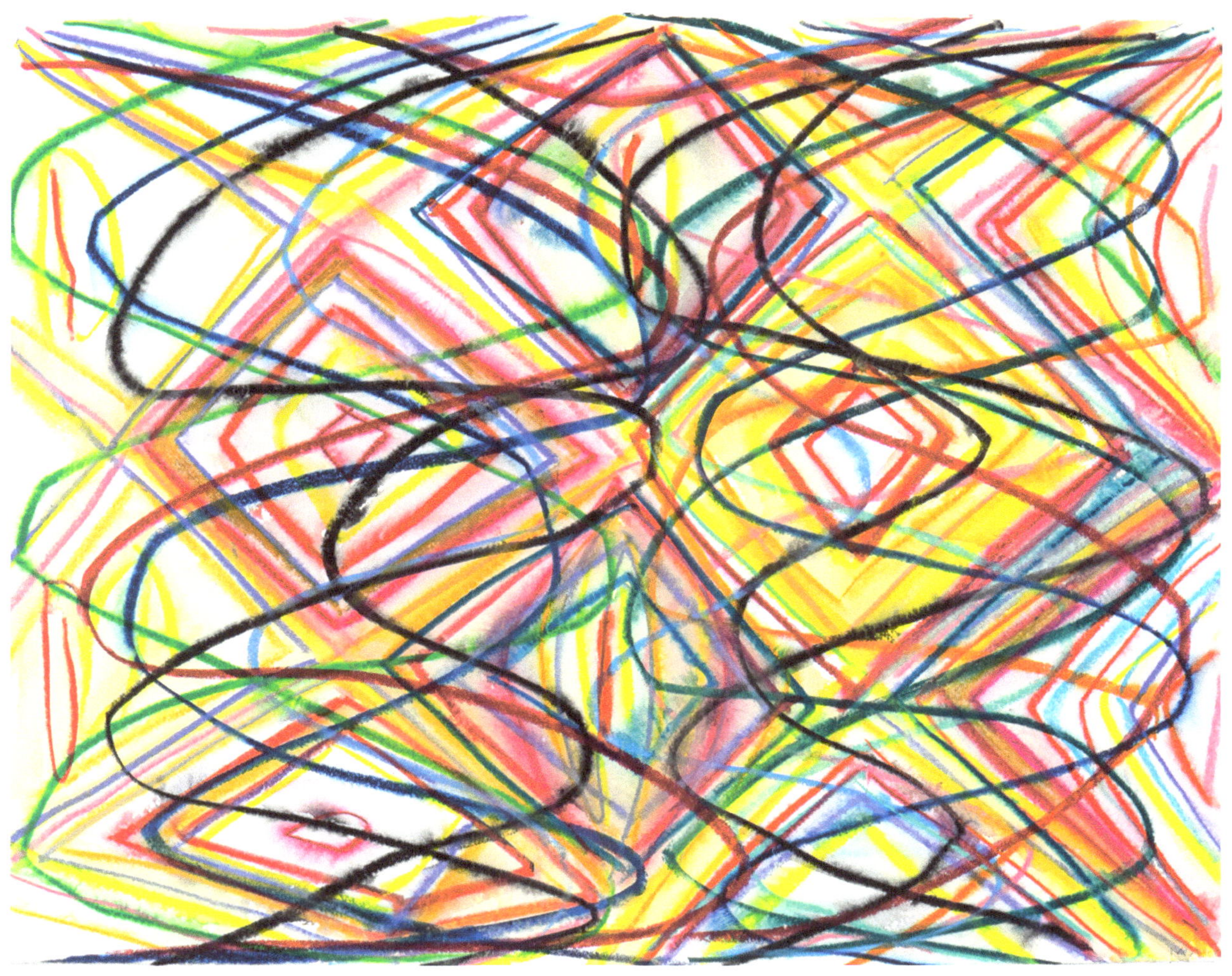

2020 #2 water-soluble crayon on paper 20 x 25 in.
Courtesy of the artist and Salon 94, New York.

Üla Einstein

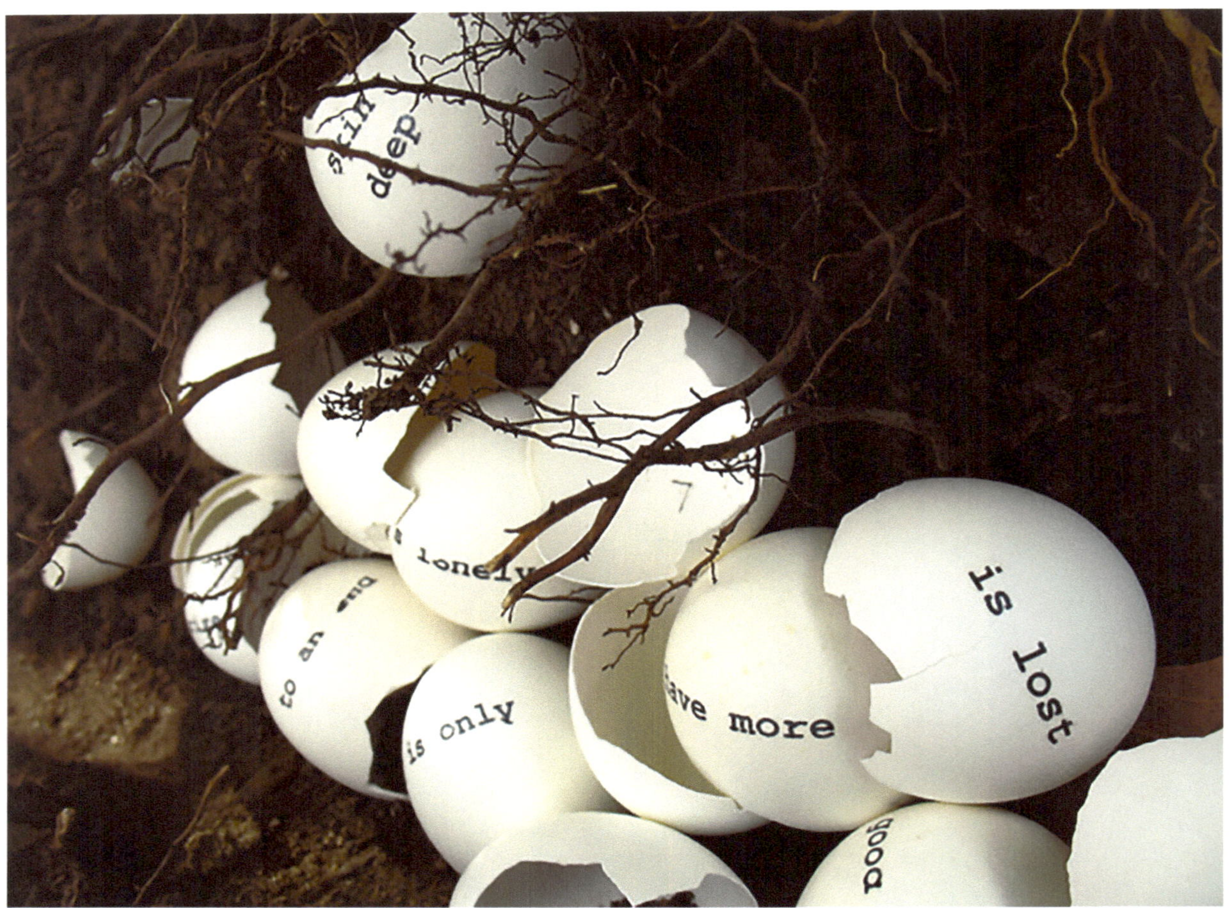

Early Influences temporary installation, limited edition C-Prints. text, broken shells

Only In Stacking Books Can The Tree Feel Its Weight Again

I am so fucking sick of nations
and the men who love them
the number of suicides
this afternoon hiding
in bottom of a cup
I feel feral out here
found a man who likes me like that
found a man who lives the way I do
7 years on the road anniversary soon
you only have to destroy
yourself for love until it is normal
which makes love normal
and refuse to live a day without it
an inferno if it
at 16 sleeping with
my mother's boyfriend
I was overwhelmed with it
solids form around you until you
struggle no more beneath it
feel throat open in a word
naming new stars moving across
the ceiling from the disco ball
constellations with stories to
soften hardened hearts
we finish the night
reading poetry out loud
last night Erica Kaufman's
mind blowing Post Classic
poetry and love
sure know how to
hang a Welcome sign out
measure and transmit from
the pink and adorable telemetry
no more waiting between parenthesis
we now excel in the ether while holding hands

Elisabeth Workman

Cleft Figure

Heraclitus might
have said War
is father of all
king of all
then slit the
neck of a lesser
at the company pic
nic of the patriarchy
while — in another
construct —
Hera, Queen Bitch
(sometimes called
quote Cow Face unquote
according to Greek
godsandgoddesses
dot net), in a
given ecstasy
could have said
You know
I could crush
your precious head
with my heifer
thighs and devour
you but did
not and did
not her omission
noted here from
this nether world
neither heaven
nor civilized
but heavily branded
and still divided by
a confusion of
who consumes
vs. who's consumed
— is that
what's meant
by world
order—an ancient
formula thru which
fear is cleaving
& scapegoats
— cloven

The City

in august 2020 birds got fat
they started turning back into dinosaurs
they didn't miss people

rats on the other hand missed restaurants
the better ones reviewed in the times
there are so many rat snobs

in the infernal month of august 2020
the birds and the rats compete for the future

we humans developed a dream life
that features either wings or fur

in the morning
we shower put on work clothes
and walk into the next room
to work on self-erasure

day and night mean little nows
are shaking the jello cube of time

at night me and my friend
jump over walls after putting
phosphorous on our hands

we escape from people
we meet a masked subway rat named Henna
at midnight on the bowery

we discuss astrophysics
sometimes we roll a ball of dark energy
on the rails of an empty train

and then lie down somewhere in the city

Steve Dalachinsky

doowop groove

chi bot shi bop
wo oh chi bop shi bop
whoa ohhhh
so crowded ya can't go anywhere
why'nt ya go to the cemetery
he says
grandma's there
grandpa
dad
brother
mom — aunts uncles
friends acquaintances
rich folk & poor
suckers
sounds crowded there too
i says
it's up to stairs & down 3
then out the open opera
i only have eyes for you but can't remember
where or when or even the hell you are
peeled & one-stopped
a backyard is after all a backyard
jus'ask yer local pawnbroker
too live too staged
put out pretty petty another time
40 dark pills
lips pursed & waiting
gone badly treated softening rocks
pale cave dwellers piping pink noise
like a bottle of sirens / roost
complaints compliant w/holding floods

did this sky hold high above itself
above our creamed soup
then opening like an eye   un helped
heep upon itself — taxing?
itself by breath & sounds
fast & out of...............................
lost inside shi bot shoo bop shooo bot shi bop shooobopshi-
bop.

zeena/phobia (the music of Zeena Parkins)

day 1

a.

this tremendous output from inside
no caca/phon(e)y
institute radical collaborations
sense the sense-say-tions
much continuous energy / motion
there is so much more behind this
power we are hearing
myriads of collective dynamisms
distant sirens blend with &
echo simultaneous evocations
almost too good not to be criminal

let me concentrate on the mastery
rather than dissect it.

b.

intimate distances & frenzy
even when one's own sound
is lost within the sounds of others
the tension lost within the sonorities
the language barriers blur
within the disruption
the music erupts then melts
as it softens & flows
toward the next faultline's genesis
this ever-increasing adventure
& risk
totally stoned on commit-
ment
reminder & expectation
renewal & relevance
connection & dissolution
passion in its extreme
but let my mind become the music
rather than letting the music
become my mind.

—— dalachinsky nyc the stone 9/10/19

from Alphaville Revisited

Wrong World
I've been working on a
unified theory
to make sense of my
uncertain perspective
in a universe 14.8 billion
years old, to concatenate
the vectors.
You know: Alonso hits
a ball to the right side,
the grinding of stone
down in the air shaft,
the moment of this pen
on paper making
thoughts tangible.

*

Fishing Line
Fishing line.
Amazing, right?

*

Tomorrow's headlines today
Poet Topples Trump
Earth Renamed Rolling Stone

*

For those with intention but little talent
Who am I to judge?
Get up on that stage.
Leave me out of it

*

I used to recant
now I decant

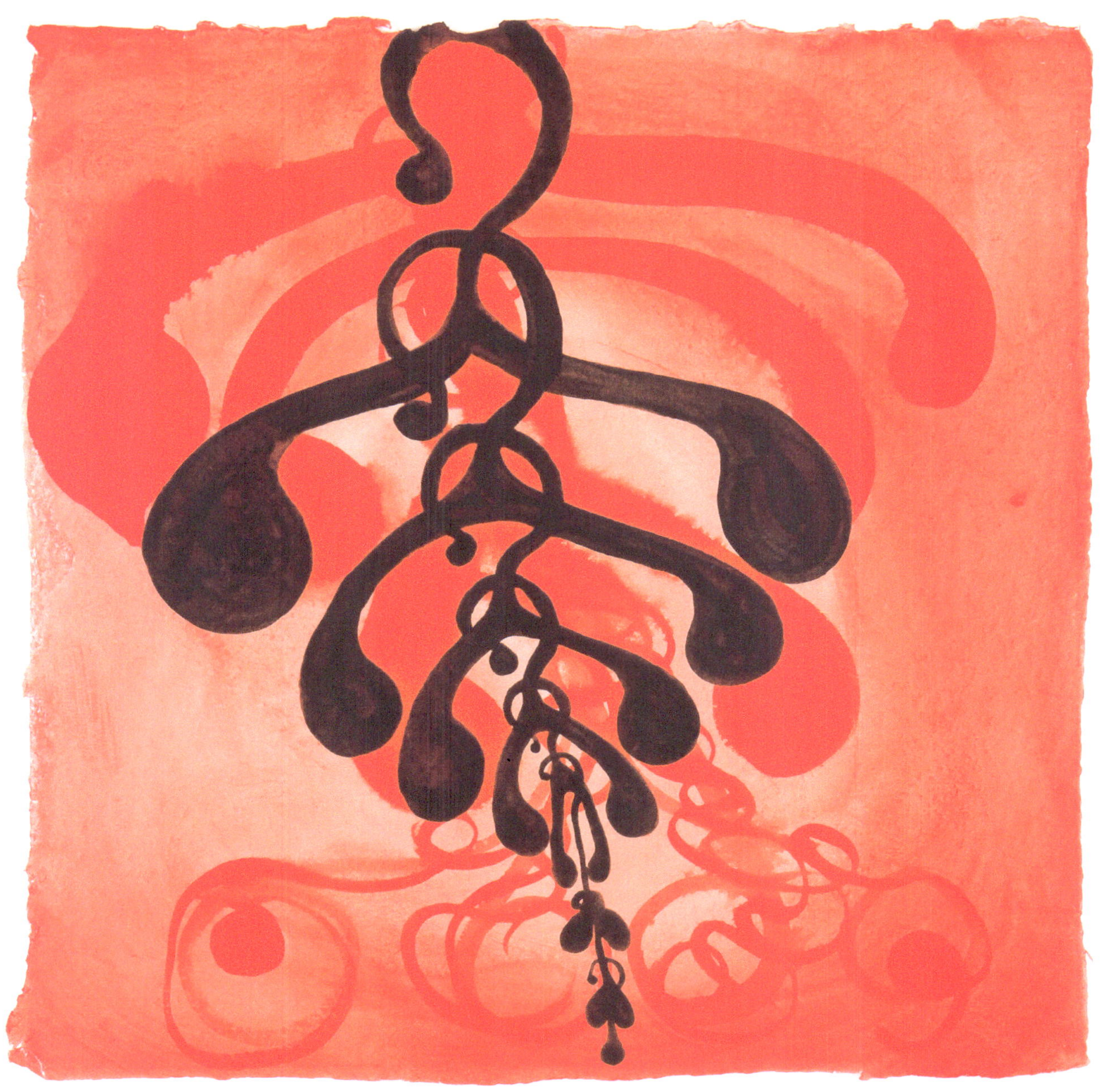

Survival #2, 2020 acrylic on khadi paper 12 x 12 in.

Patricia Spears Jones

Walking on Avenue A on the Tompkins Square Park Side

We are walking Sandra Payne and me on an unpeopled Avenue A.

It is dark but too dark and even in the daytime, it's dark on Avenue A.

We walk on the sidewalk on the Tompkins Square Park side, no dogs

We see Steve Cannon driving a sedan. He rolls down his window

Want a ride? Sandra waves no, But I say hey he may be going further,

So we go over to where he is parking his car. It's 7th Street — he parallel parks

On Avenue A & 7th Street so the garage man can check his car.

This is the unblind Steve, the un-glasses Steve, his eyes bright brown

but what is strange is his hair. He has too much straight black hair.

It's a wig, a sort of bad Beatles cut with bangs. Steve Cannon with bangs.

He's smiling but the hair, it's post chemo wig hair. It's the worst haircut

you've ever had and must cover it up wig hair. Steve had that New Orleans

Mess with me hair. The wig is rebuke of all that New Orleans flare.

Steve smiles, patient with the garageman. His ride is a Volvo?

It's roomy and safe and he salutes Sandra and me and we salute him back

And then the dream ends

SOCIAL DISTANCING

There is nothing more American than making choices for others.

Human weakness is the greatest business opportunity there ever was.

To state the obvious, an epidemic had to arrive from somewhere.

A world populated by selfish and ignorant people out for their own gain rather than
acting for the common good.

The butchery of animals was likely to produce fetid air.

He was arrested, punished and sent to the secret prison.

The family was instinctively suspicious of me.

Once the plague had taken hold, the influence of the health and disease of the citizenry
on the body of the state was used as a justification to take measures against the poorer
members of society.

He was evidently a disruptive character.

We live with the greatest fear.

POSSESSION WITH INTENT TO DISTRIBUTE

The story is a first-person narrative with no more than a few phrases of reported speech,
strong on atmosphere and situation, low on incident.

Much of what we know as modern politics.

Other white men adhered to a stoic and lonely individualism.

Each rubbing the other the right or wrong way.

Self-help gurus warn against getting too wrapped up in other people's problems.

Revolution as a leap into the future.

Not exactly the house one would choose for calming one's nerves.

There are godly and demonic spheres, labyrinths, palaces, gateways guarded by terrifying
gatekeepers, manic buzzes and hums, disorienting temporal rhythms, and hosts of
musicians, some ominous, others benign.

I've got to get some rest; that's all I'm trying to express.

A simpleton who was not cut out for the role that he wanted to play.

One of a multitude of riveting figures.

Yes, I've plenty of stories to tell, but one mustn't tell everything one knows.

I actually groaned with anguish.

They expected things to turn out worse.

The orchestra refused to stop.

Carl Hazlewood

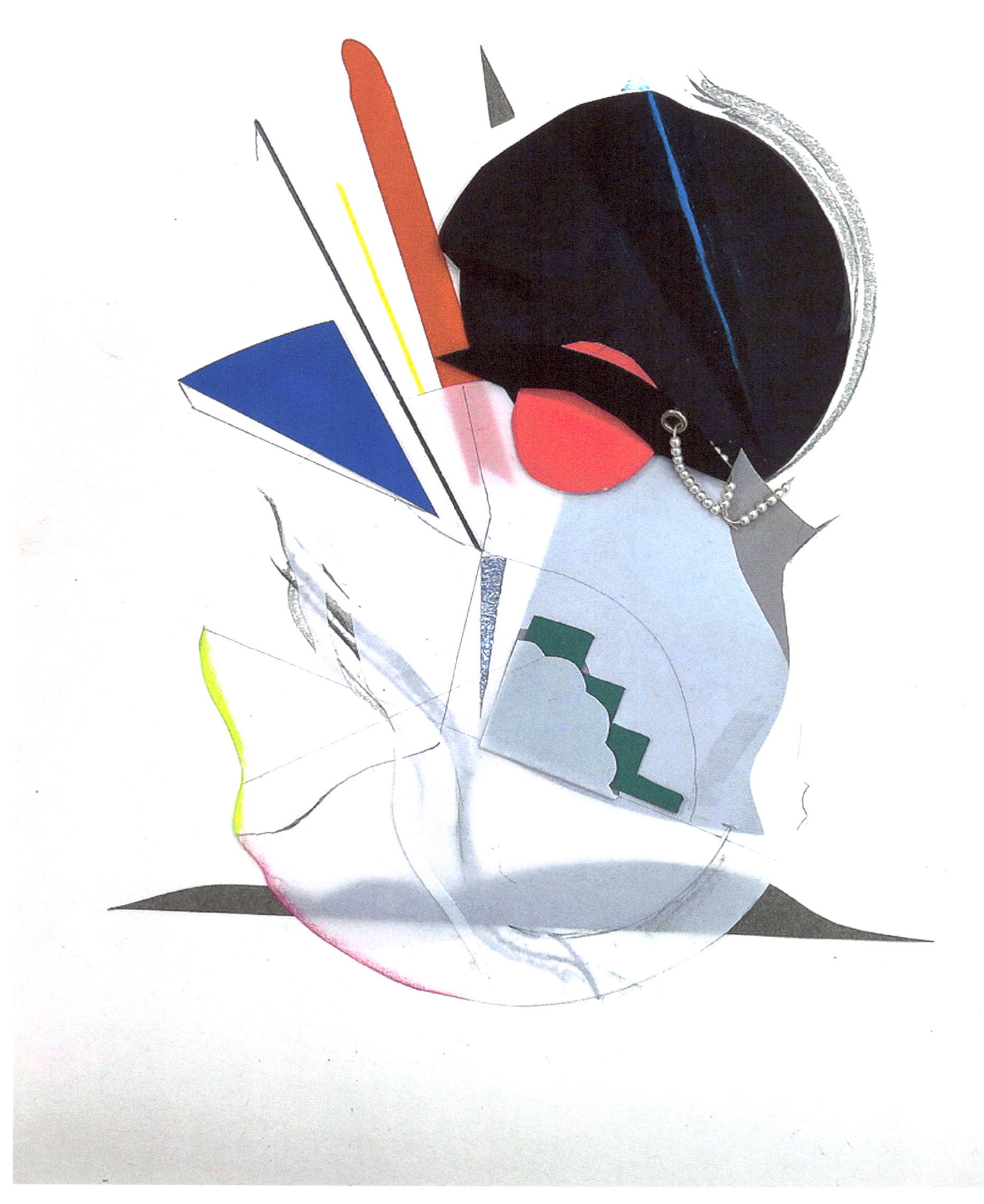

BlackHead Laughter 2016
Cut archival papers, graphite, vinyl tape,pastel, coloured pencil, fake pearls
20 x 16 in. Courtesy June Kelly Gallery, NYC

16

Made in America

If I were a less sane person I would probably stalk
Zoey Deschanel. After stalking her from nine to five,
I would come back home to my wife and daughter
and tell them about my day. "I stalked Zoey, but I

never saw her," I'd say. "You're just not trying hard
enough," my wife would reply, "don't give up." After
glaring at me for a moment my daughter would say,
"Why don't you just find a real job? No one's going

to pay you to stalk Zoey Deschanel." So I'll tell her
about fame, about the things in this world that aren't
real and the rain and the empty river in a dream. "I'm
not doing this for money," I'll explain, and she'll turn

away from me and back to her strawberries, pulling
a plump red cone from the blue bowl on the table.

COFFEE LINE

The coffee line in front of me
as I wait for milk to reach
the right temperature.
It will be cold where I'm
going, snowflakes like sequins
pressed to the scarf.

In the coffee line
I see his gold tooth
glisten with his happiness.
It is then that I want to
steal it, show him the transparent
look of sadness.

Leaving behind the coffee line
I unravel everything.
He is thinking about paella
and language. I am planning
my escape, but no matter
how much I undo
there is always more to bind me.

Another coffee line
in breaks from the library,
studying Apollinaire.
I wish I still had those pages,
responsible for my unraveling.
Put the pieces together.
I am no longer trudging through snow,
foaming milk.

Remembrance

The dead have taught me
that I am alive through them,
in their dust I inhale,
in the water that seeps through the soil
and reaches my throat.
They brush by me in gusts of wind,
speak to me in ancient tongues,
and in their silence.
They seem more present now
than when they were in bodies,
for being everywhere
and nowhere.
Are they still real?
How gone are they?
What difference…
those beneath the earth,
those above still plotting.

Night Vision

Some men lace in
on you like
a long trumpet note
in an igneous grey three AM
club cloud
beyond the fourth bourbon,
gauze in your eyes
toothy glints of promise
canceling danger.
You ride it
like a surfer
on dusty shafts
before light arrives
slanting in subtly
between slats
in the blinds
breaking up
night vision
now caught in
that dry space
between the tongue
and hope.

Daniel Rosenbaum

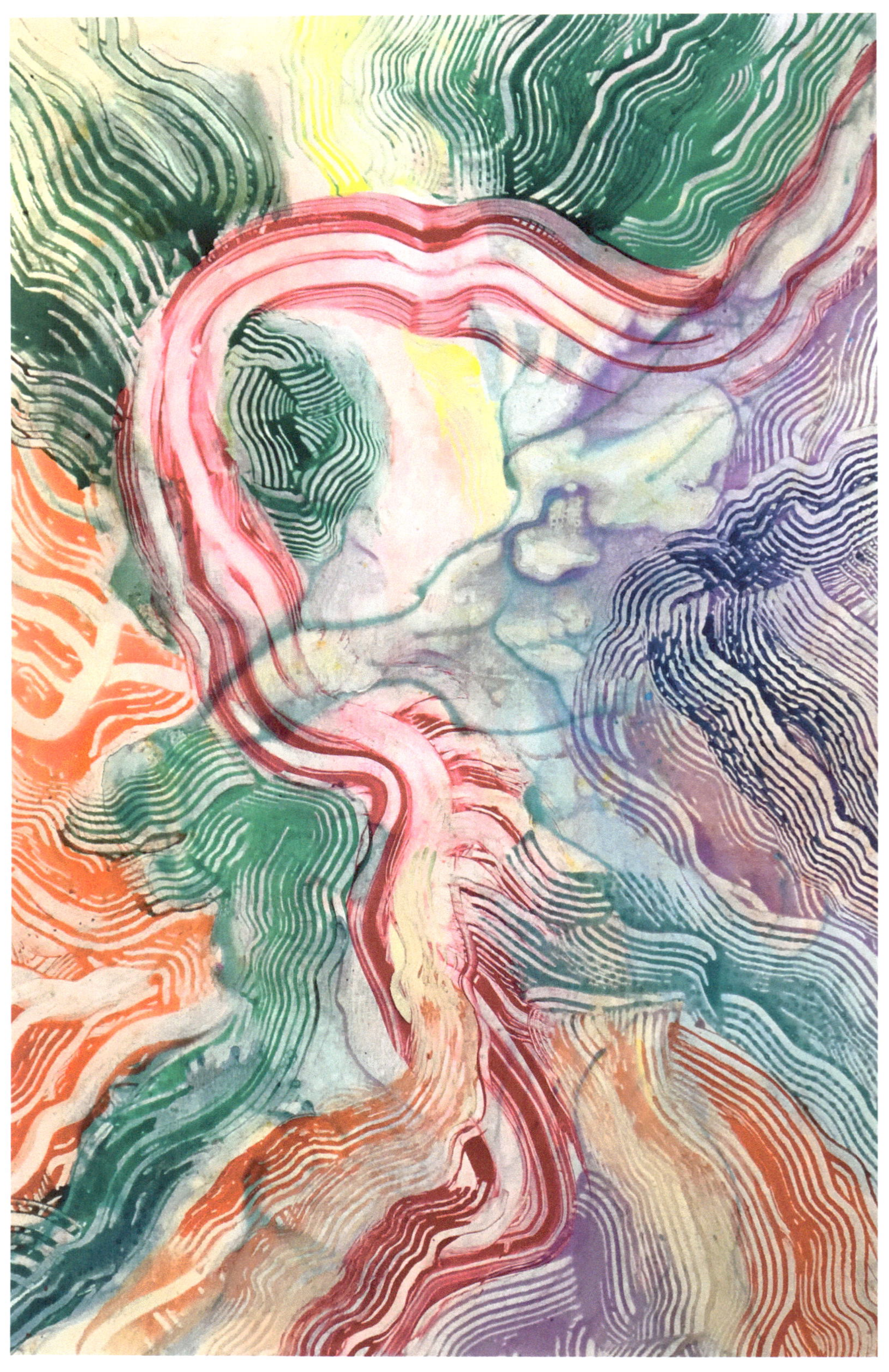

Topo-Boy 2019 Acrylic on canvas 60 x 40 in.

Everywhere in Paris

Street signs on the sides of buildings
Remind me history is as close as
Someone smoking a cigarette, eating
A baguette, or walking three dogs on the sidewalk,
But at eight-thirty in the morning
I don't care. I order a second
Cappuccino and read an e-mail
From someone who writes, "You should
Go to a famous café, take out a notebook and pen,
And see what happens."
So far, nothing has happened,
Except the crumbs from my croissant
Are staining the pages of my notebook,
And a woman with a large leather bag
Has taken off her coat and sat down next to me.
Le Hibou isn't famous like The Ritz, The Dome,
Or Café de Flore, where tourists now sit at those
Still famous tables.
But I like this café better as I write
My fabled, Paris history on a postcard to
A friend in New Jersey:
"I have discovered a place to hang out,
And on my second day here
I have a date tonight."

Ed Sanders

Time-Tithing

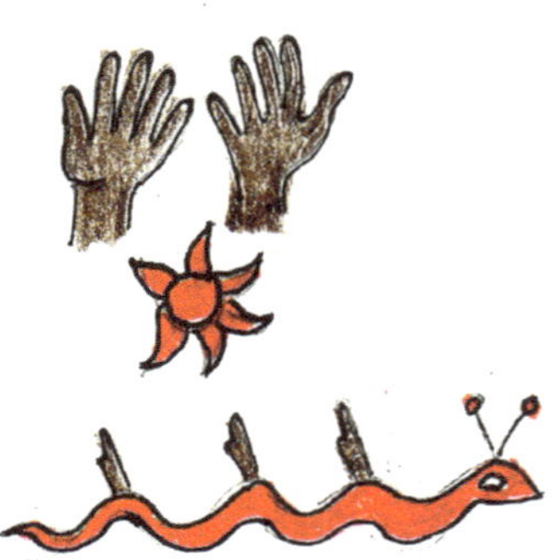

What's a Sunflower to do
surrounded by Millions of Suns?
or what's a human to do
surrounded by thousands of causes,
injustices, ridiculous wars,
a new generation of nuclear bombs
dead honey bees, poisoned water,
stifling air, the shiny eyes of
starvation and poverty?

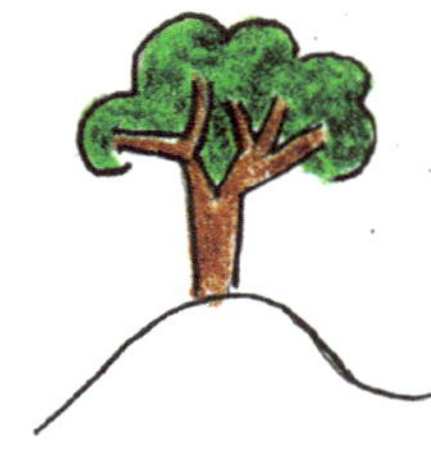

What to do? What to do?

You can't live continuously
in a Down Zone

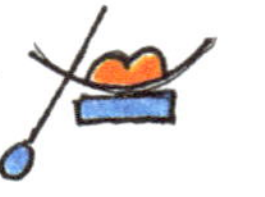

You need to take time for fun
even with a cancer ward
just miles away

The answer is to
Tithe your Time
work work work
on a regular schedule
pick some causes
and tithe your time
take risks
Tithe Your Time
confront the evil
Tithe Your Time
work work work
on a regular schedule
Tithe Your Time
Tithe Your Time
ten percent of it
Every Single Day
Tithe Your Time

Nagasaki Day 2020

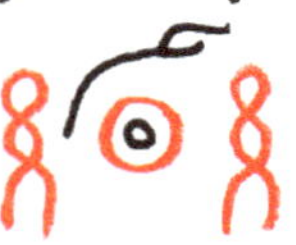

Edward Sanders
August 9, 2020

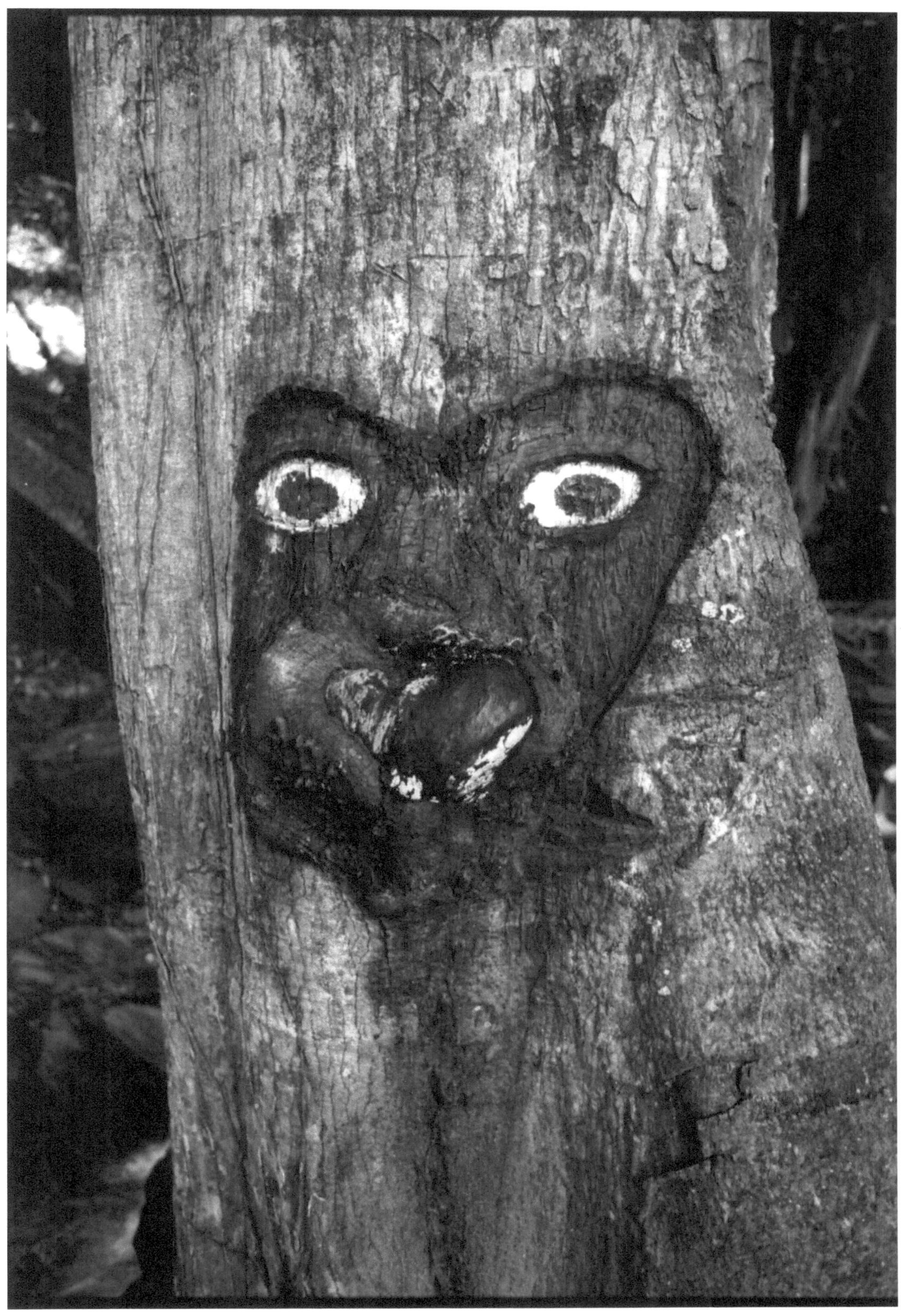

Pablo Delano, *Tree Carving, Orisha Shrine, Blue Basin,*
Diego Martin, Trinidad and Tobago, 2003, silver gelatin print

David Mills

We Are
(The Covid pandemic)

We are a Queens-bred Italian-
American governor straightening
the state's spine. Daily. We are
an African-American borough
president from Brooklyn handing
out gloves to black folks who are
falling farthest and fastest (13%
of the nation; 50% of the corpses)
We are a mask mailed to the Apple
from a white, Kansas farmer who'd never
left his state's wheat fields: its flat
rectangular majesty; we are a Nigerian
home health aide (an essential worker)
who speaks broken English but, with
kindness, fixes up her clients, a Salvadoran
home health aide who speaks little English
but gives buckets of love. We are comfort
from a ship with the same name; we are
12,000 medical personnel who came
to an Apple being eaten alive, chewed
up and spit out by something invisible
and insidious, but we/they came with-
out question, with or without fear
(sometimes without a hotel room)
but with hearts that beat determined
to beat back a virus. We are a Mexican
delivery boy who died with his family
south of the border and he, caught in
New York's essential slaughterhouse,
buried in an anonymous carton in Hart
Island's potter's field. America is a Bronx
sanitation worker headed back to hauling
trash after a hip replacement. America is
a doctor who was stricken by the invisible
but rose again to give her life to those on
ventilators only to sadly take her own
life because she could take it no longer:

patients who, if lucky, died with only
a stranger's hand to hold. We are a Native
American community that asked for medical
supplies but were sent body bags. We are a 28-
year-old Navajo who now wanders among covid's
ghosts, leaving behind a two-year-old daughter
named Poet whose arteries pump metaphors
rather than blood. America is a prayer, is
an hour that applauds every day, is 7 p.m.
resounding so loud it's rattling heaven's gates.
America is now this uninvited hour we will
somehow get through.

Talking to the Teeth

(Teeth of enslaved New Yorkers found in
     Manhattan's slave cemetery, 18th century)

Now you are one with a skull: its white hush
     But sometimes a mouth was a hot leaking
     cottage we was all forced to live in

Front tooth, why were you whittled to an enamel fang?
     Animal fang? What animal?

Not animal. Enamel. Teeth ingredients. like what you been
reduced to: bone
     When she giggled. chewed or smiled, some knew
     I might be the one thing she clung to from home.

In the children's graves, their teeth were almost always gone
     Cause they was the here-born. The start
     life. The too-often sugar, corn suppers.

In the back of your mouth, one of you looks like a peg.
     Death picks everything clean. Here now,
     skinned, buried, lips can no longer
     hush us, way a lid might muffle
     a pot of cornmeal mush.

And, you, tooth, shaped like an hourglass?
     A tooth occasionally tells a skull's time: means I was
     born and adorned before this unwelcoming earth.

Carolanna Parlato

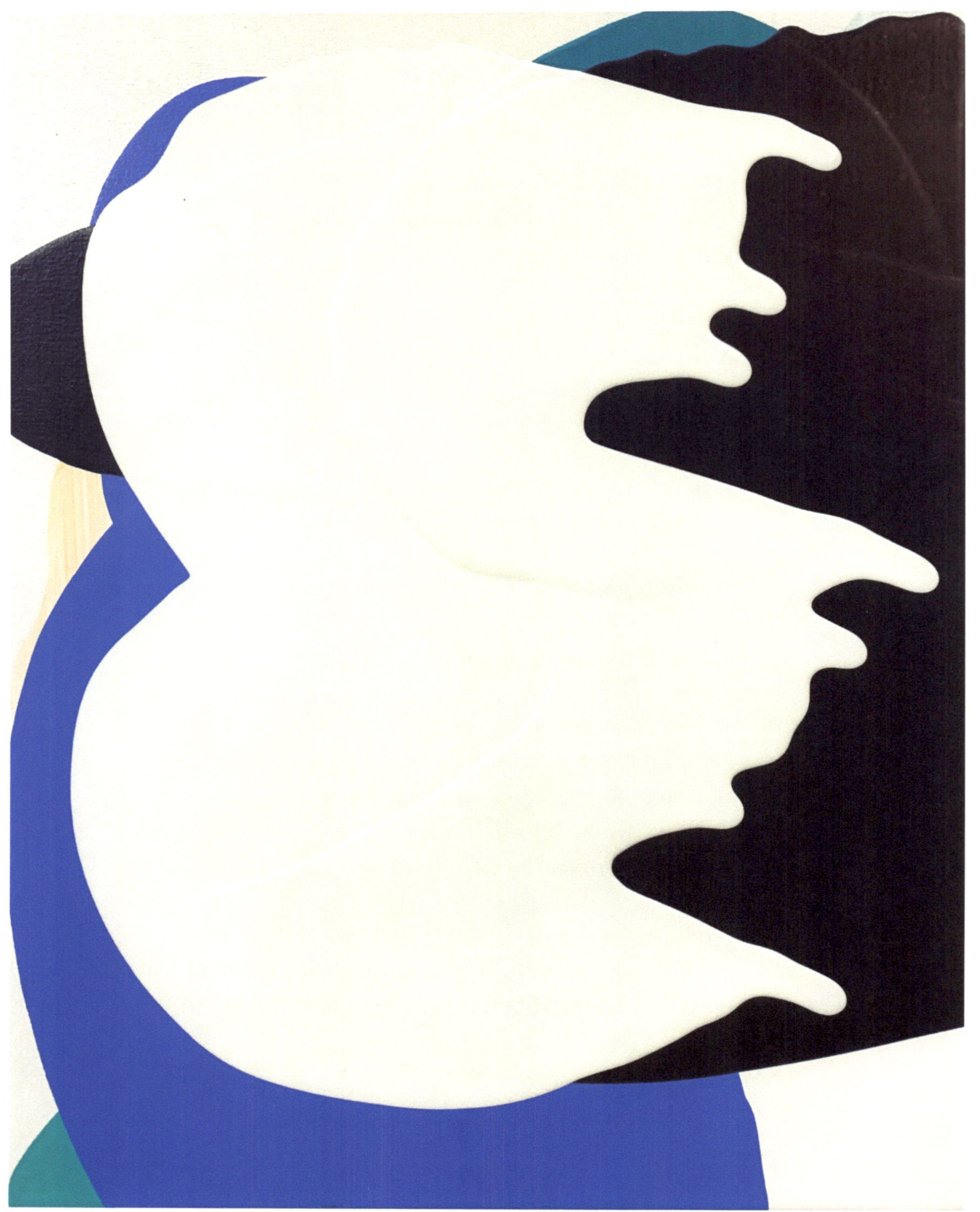

Slider 2019 acrylic on canvas 16 x 12 in.

Ego conquiro

The question?

The encounter with the un-
known
that distorts the myth
about its
victims

an apparatus that
singularly
desires to pretend that
the other was myself.

For this,
to submit
and conquer
with disgrace

to a being that
is not a being
of the world
I know of.

Its dominance
leads it
to forget
its root

and projects me
as a
perpetrator
in his error,

integrating it
into the appropriate,
the civil,
the correct.

There is no
valid
excuse.

There is
no response
for the soulless.
It proceeds from
modern life
period.

To be,
think
and act.

To me it seems
that
we have

focused
enough,
too much
to remain.

We have enlightened
ourselves in the shadow
of an emptiness
and stopped.

We have
fed ourselves with greed
and entanglements

to dazzle
with the shadow
a conquest,
a failure.

The lilies
that were
affirming themselves

break from their
beginnings
their remoteness,

their corpses
that arise
from streams

to affirm
this same
permanence.

They have
disappointed us
up to here
with trivialities

that enrich
irises
and daisies.

Nothing
there are other
furrows

truncated
by sun in the
water

and the strong
who line up for
the search

from
there
to here

And there
power
to become.

There
power to be.

There
power to be aware.

There
power
to have knowledge.

Ilka Scobie

Home

When we speak of home,
metaphors careen from square footage
to familial longing
From real estate envy
to yearning for a room of one's own.

In a settler's nation,
cities rise upon stolen lands,
Home-less-ness equates
those without shelter as less than
those for whom a key unlocks
a personal place, somewhere safe

Home, like love can be elusive
Expensive, exhausting,
exhilarating, existential,
Home as habitat, haven
Nomad's respite
Nester's retreat
During a pandemic, where we go to isolate
During sleep, so nightmares can turn to dreams.

To Grow Old

This body, in which we live
An instrument of pleasure
to give and receive
this heart, these eyes, our feet
and hands
taken for granted, as the rising sun

We begin, smooth fleshed with strong teeth
Heart caged in protective bone
No matter, how or where we live
Our bodies are our home

We smoke, we drink, carelessly copulate
We drug, we abuse, we play with fate
When young, experience is what we crave
To grow old, you must be lucky and brave

Courtyard Night

for Ilka Scobie

I can't bear to remember
What I'm unable to forget.
The hem of the green
Curtain lifted, just enough
To show between the legs
Of the room.
The bed undone, rumpled,
Stained with lamp light.
Day peers in, leers, waits.
Then, night
Like a beat cop chases
The perv off. And by
An adjusting hand, the curtain
Drops, the hand vanishes inside and
Her moans fill the courtyard.
My dog and I in our own lonely
Dark, lie awake, listening, Miles Davis
On, his piercing horn, and from
The window across the way
The woman's
Wet piercing cries.
I have sometimes seen her
Leave the building. She
Has clever eyes. I can imagine
Her face, tortured by pleasure.
I can imagine what he is doing,
And close, and close,
And close
Myself
Off.

There Are More Important Things Than Living: A Checklist

1. A girl who poops
2. Doing the whole Manhattan/Long Island/Westchester Jew thing in one year
3. muff-check at the door
4. King Lear — bitches all over his boar tusks
5. a kitten archbishop
6. bestiality suede + contravariant bagel circumcision = crabs my other fetish
7. Gender issues, girls, private parts, questions, students
8. It's all about the facials, but it's also about Chuck Norris
9. operation hobbitporn
10. Hello! Hot Asian girl, listening to iPod in Penn Station
11. a tampon to stick anywhere
12. King Kong and dinosaurs fighting even though they are from different centuries and I don't even believe in dinosaurs.
13. sell mangina, WalMart patdown?
14. Here's a hint: passive voice. Here's another: barn did not fall down
15. dog arms bailout, but not frog or clown
16. dick liquor
17. being watched by a fear duck
18. What's in a Caesar salad? Ya'll know about it?
19. elevator, Pratt Institute, zombies, Taco Bell, dolphin
20. I can float, but I don't have big boobs
21. bottle rocket skills
22. a sad puppy that burps
23. Shorter older chesty woman over 45
24. Aldi's free spider with bananas offer
25. chemical spill in thunderbolt autopussy
26. Sure, it's promising plural dicks and that they'll be torpedo-sized, but it's not like they explode or anything.
27. Naked teens attacking home detector over a simple case of snowball testicle
28. OMG the Nazis have Hamburglar orgasms
29. Understand that my life was suxxx before
30. <pickle>
31. The team of superheroes you only call when all the other ones are busy: Can the Secret Monsterdicks help you?
32. "Quarantine, like America, is the best" (Jerry Abejo)
33. degrees

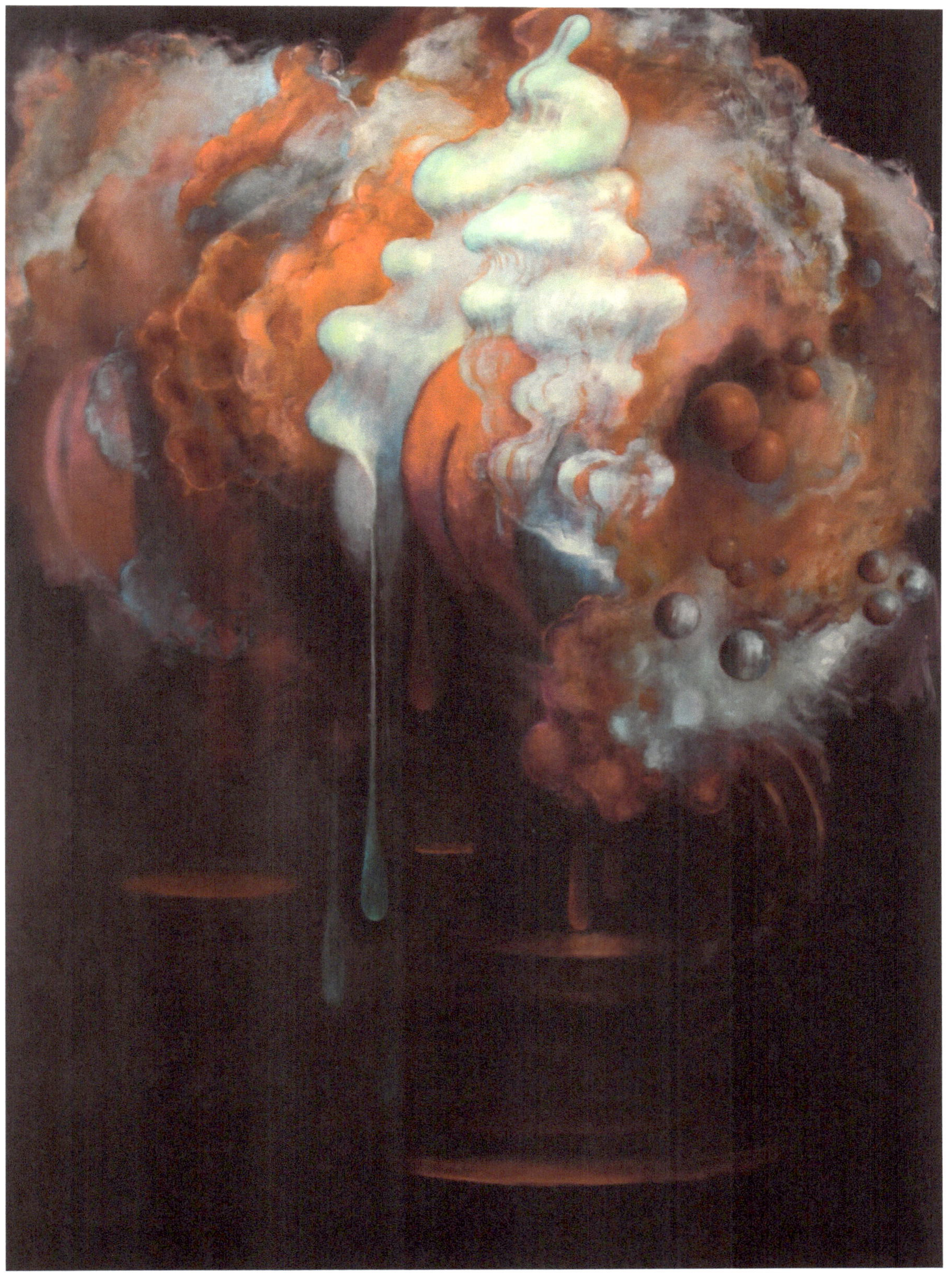

Cloud Lick 2019 oil on panel 32 x 44 in.

Cindy Hochman

Inner Life (With Sabotage)

This poem will be intentionally vague.

Candle wicks flicker. Chemicals misfire. Crossed wires refuse to untangle.

Sometimes I slip into something less comfortable.

Carousel horses and streetlights make me weep deeply.

My handsome father's death has turned into stilted breath.

My benevolent brother's death is still caught in my throat.

Everyone gives me flowers to fill the fissure between limbs and loss.

And I bury them under layers of, what? Nothing but my own undoing.

A startled and startling voice tells me to go even deeper than this.

Onyx and obsidian wrestle it out with a chest full of white diamonds.

Frankly, my dear, I've had enough of dancing through the murk with my not-so-better angels.

Excuse me while I remove this battering ram from my solar plexus.

Let me open my palms to the hazy sunshine. I promise I will stop shaking soon.

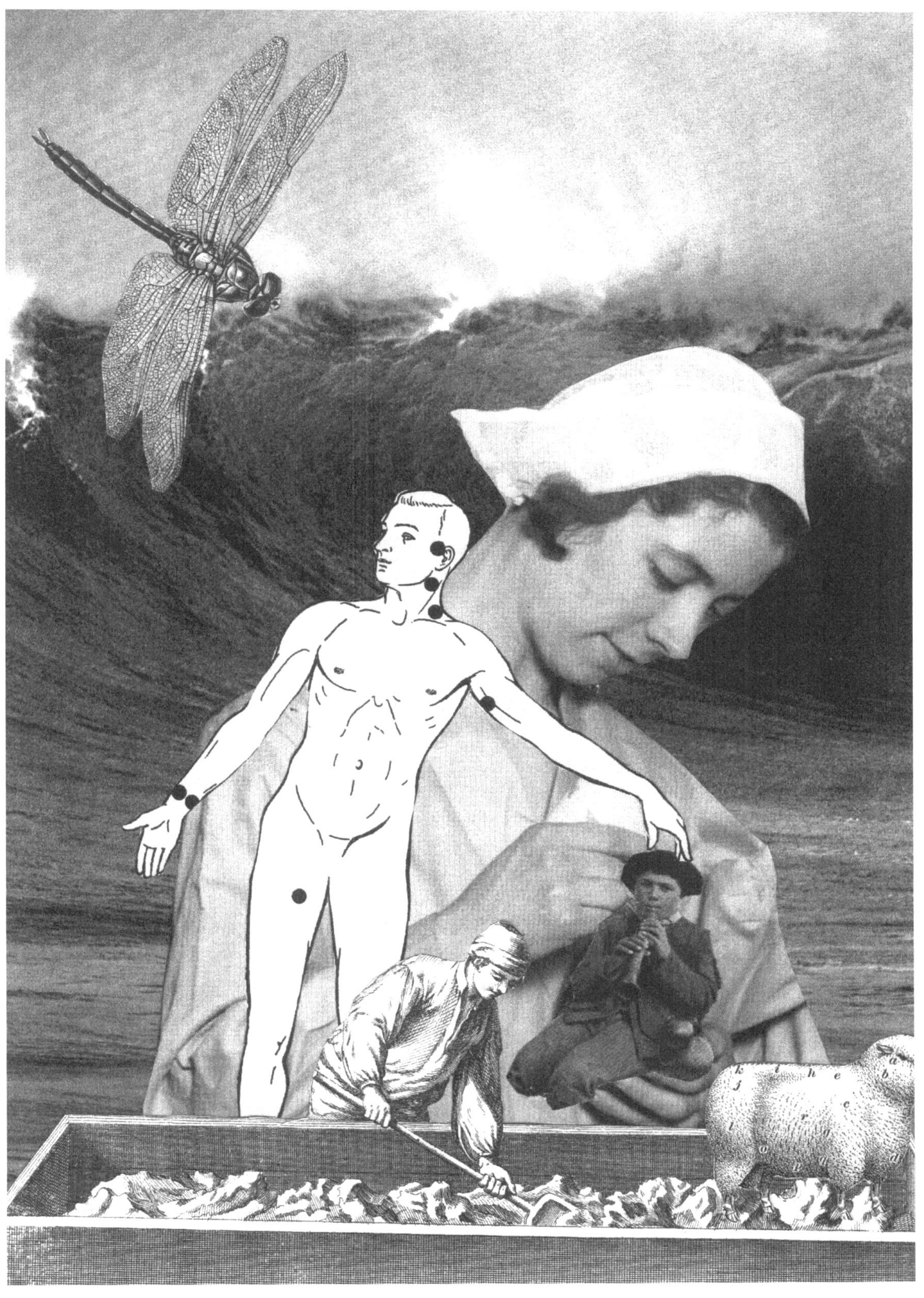

The Arrival (IV) 2018 collage 10 ¼ x 7 ¾ in.

John J. Trause

Endangered Generation: Hanging On

How should this pretty scary tale begin
of how coronavirus came about?
Behold the pretty scaly pangolin:
prehensile-tailed and with ant-eating snout,
carnivorous, that's insects mostly, kin
to true anteaters and nocturnal too,
with imbricated scales of keratin,
so prized in China, but who can know who
in Wuhan, Hubei, first ran foul of that
poor pangolin, down on its luck and bit
by that odd batshit crazy horseshoe bat
to render pandemonium, COVID-
19, that caused the death, as this tale spins,
of humans and endangered pangolins.

Hopeless Cases

are Zen Buddhism,
Picasso (except for a few pieces that are nostalgic for me,
only a tiny portion of his massive splooging),
Rembrandt,
Rilke (in German and English translation),
Aristotle's Poetics (in Greek and English translation),
Cy Twombly (except for the sculptures,
one "Rococo" room in the Twombly Annex of the Menil Collection,
and some late drip paintings),
Jazz, the Blues,
Ingmar Bergman,
Richard Dreyfuss before Down and Out in Beverly Hills,
Philip Seymour Hoffman (except in Boogie Nights and The Talented Mr. Ripley),
eggnog, pound cake, tuna fish in a can, anchovies, tripe, onions, garlic,
baked beans, sauerkraut,
and mayonnaise (the Devil's spunk).

No. 183. "The Only Way to Freedom is Song"

We're stuck between Jerusalem and Athens

—

Socrates and Moses jumping up and down play-
ing double Dutch

—

with their skirts raised and lead and gold ropes in
rhythm between them sounding off

—

"finally this is this

—

it it and to accept/it this/dim screen/a baffling
means"

—

and all calles like Belfast's ghosts

—

if the dead lose their 64 names

—

intersecting (pulse) and converging (mass) at all
points one road before you moves even if in circles
alone

—

even if it is a wall with a tree thrust out a hole
you can see rebar through the floor that some-
body has dusted a part of off

—

and under broken roof under a tarp made of cam-
ouflage material's made a home to sing being on
the only way to freedom is song

—

is the sound

—

of utopia

—

Bart Plantenga

List From A Lost Surrealist

mandatory deportation
nail clipping spit out
fondle naked manikin on street [bad joke not appreciated]
piss on gravel
bullet breath [between teeth]
luger voice
wax beans [not found in wax museum]
Mickey Rooney [role not yet defined]
Hudson water [discolors skin]
beer laugh [brand not important]
she believes business card is a WOW
embarrassment is forgotten

map [color, 1978]

1. structural make-up (or fuck-up?)
2. the masked realities of pursuit (or where the hell are the deflating tires?)
3. campus pigskins
4. being an outcast on the inside
5. classic classes
6. paranoia pink or the truth about freaks
7. intellectual stimulation or beer & aunt stories eating Fritos
8. passive resistance or giving in to the no ones
9. profound thoughts locked up too long
10. superman sloppy joes miscellaneous
11. swords & pin cushions
12. poetry in the name of seriousness (unread)
13. conclusive evidence of the concluding lines
14. use colored pushpins
15. translate feelings into geography [skin conductance & heart rate into latitude & longitude]
16. arouse suspicion with mysterious word order
17. USA: foreigners called aliens in 1966

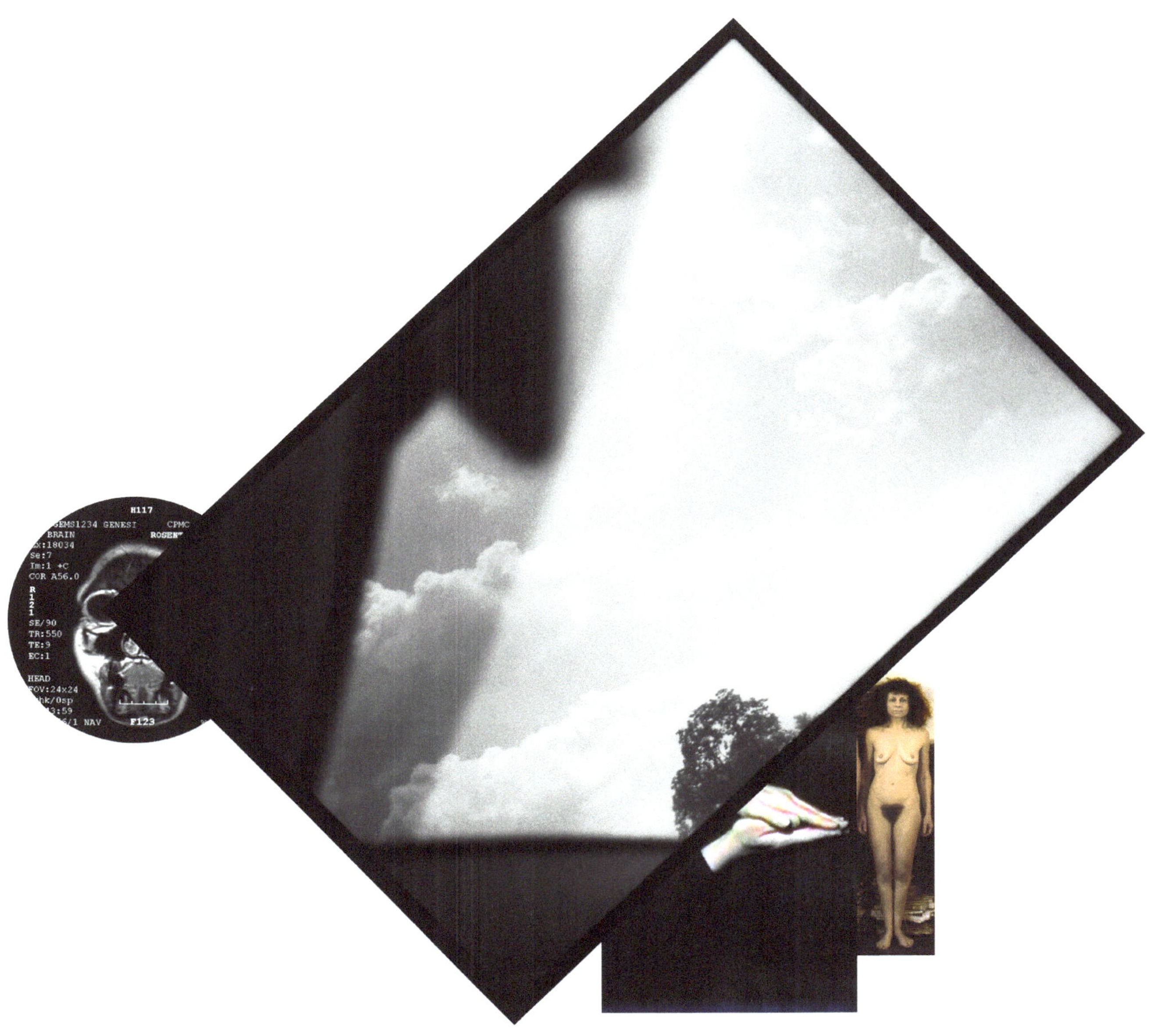

Conceptual Compositization Indiana 2006
Archival collage from digital prints of 35mm photography,
brain scan, and cropped VHS video stills;
vellum surface, variable size

AN OLD MAN LOOKS BACK ON HIS

At certain times in my life I was a handsome man.
At other times, a very goofy looking man,
a plain looking man, or an odd looking man.

I was at times an Irish-looking man
and a "white"-looking man. I often looked younger
but at times passed for older.

When asked by the director of an indie movie
to play a coked-up suicidal rabbi in it, I said
"With this Irish mug?" And he said, "The rabbi

who taught me for my Bar Mitzvah looked
exactly like you." Several times I passed for
"black" in situations, especially in the then

legally segregated South, where pale "black" folks
sometimes passed for "white" and sometimes
passed for "black" and identity seemed to be

dependent on something like mass delusion.
I've been the same weight, give or take a few
pounds, since I was fifteen, except for a few

years around age fifty where I worked out
with a trainer and bulked up with muscles
that made me feel like somebody else so

LOOKS WITH NO REMORSE

I went back to my old self and weight, though
as I grew older that weight seemed to move
around, like from my shoulders and chest to

my belly. These days as I move into my
late seventies, I seem to have acquired the
looks of a generic "old white man" indistinguishable

from other old "white" men, at least to those
who don't fit into that category, though those
of us who do can see the more subtle differences.

I could be part Jewish, or Italian, or Brazilian,
or African, or indigenous or trans or queer or
lots of things you might not think I could be

by my appearance. But what seems to matter
most to many I encounter when out in public
is that I appear to be a generic "old white man"

and from that there seems to come conclusions
I might disagree with but recognize there's no
point in doing so, minds have been made up

in most cases, and any words or gestures or
styles, or ways I can look, will not change those
conclusions. As happens to so many others.

Patricia Fabricant

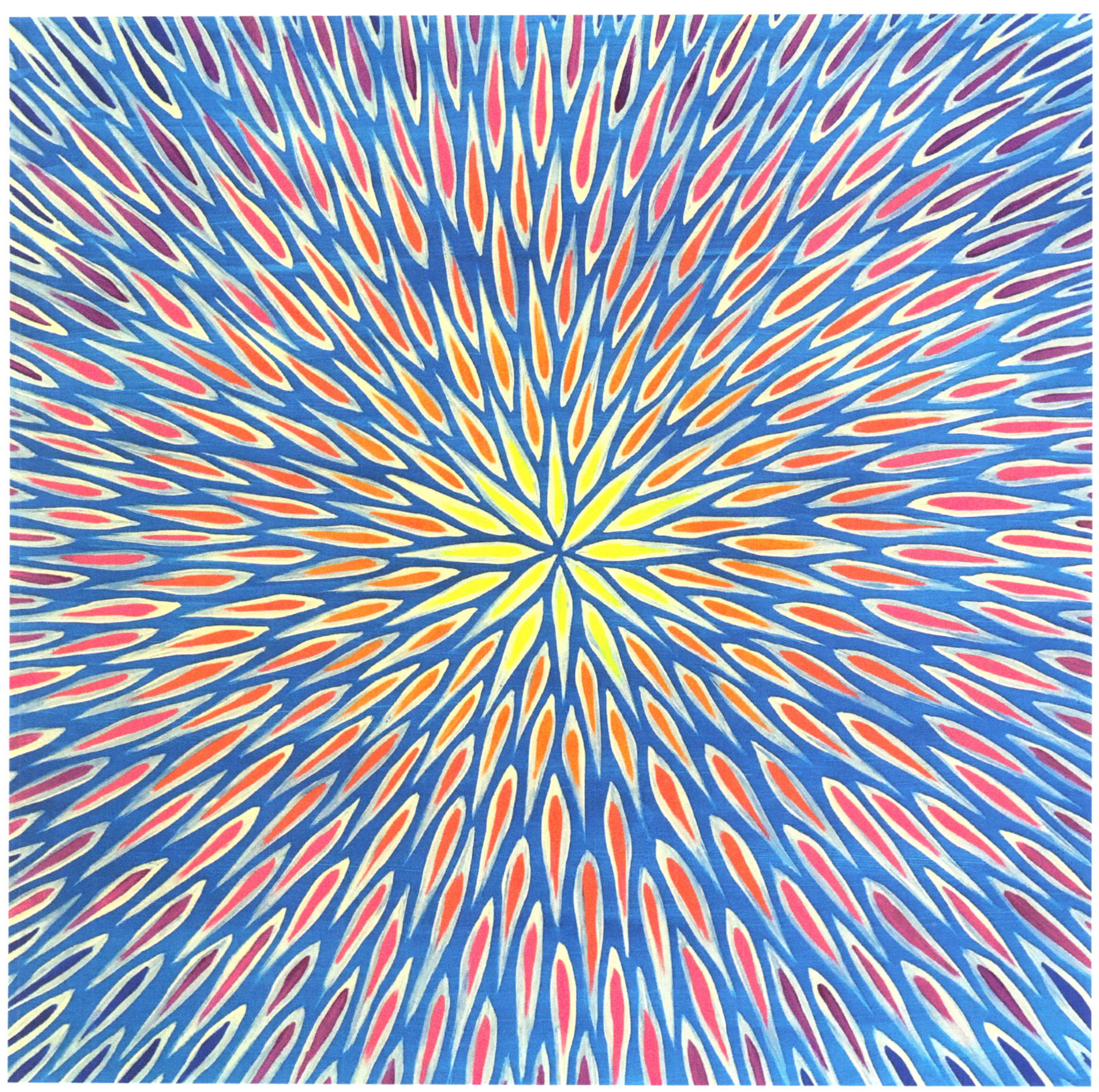

011520, 2020 gouache on panel 12 x 12 in.

CINDER BLUE

fire cruel
make believe
president's guts
in a cup of fog
your line
on the life
bird screech
Francisco San
Pedro dam
bat sparks
sanguine cypress
down your block
black mind
skull glow
oh so slow
teeth clasp
eyelids snap
violet nails
life bank
ice eyes
ferns float
Gold vomit
tear popsicle
angel beast
twisted horn
love invincible
wonder woman
death bow
plunge high
fist calm

seek mist
jaguar dance
chess king
dice roll
rock plop
ghost holy
redwoods ring
eye sky
spine strike
tendon splinter
frog mask

cabra cobre
firefly DNA
coral cut
doll awakens
corn maze
sockets empty
music rain
bone coins
soul salt

Lawrence Swan

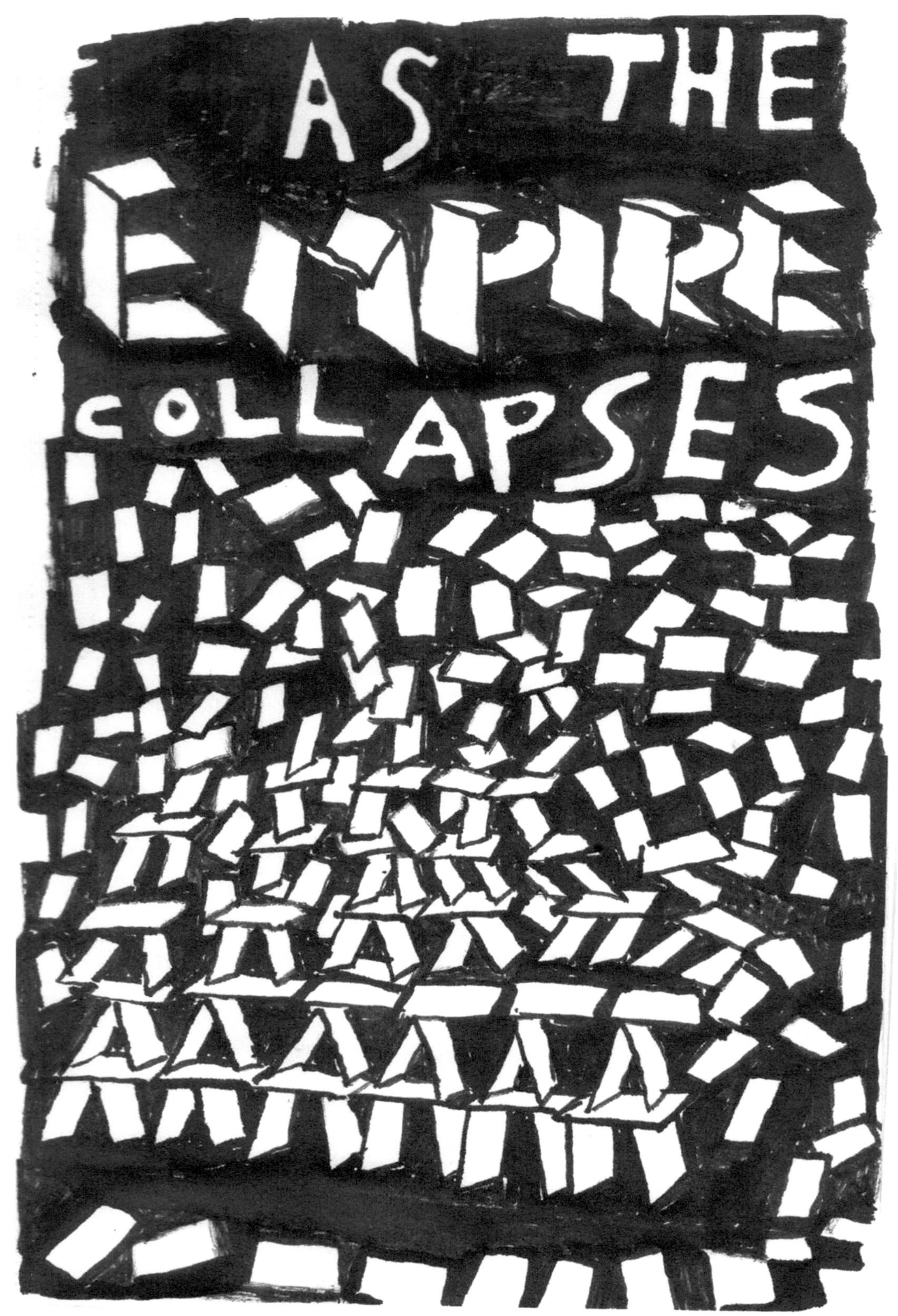

The Empire Collapses 2011 ink on paper

SHAVINGS & LOAN

Jump right in. What gives pause
is tomb-sweeping duty but duty
calls. Scramble the Phantoms.
What feels like 100 per cent is.

Maybe. Befuddled by fudge…
dithering and diddling. Fiddling
at the Fire Sale. Lonely
as a pangolin on the South Lawn.

Witness the witless grandstanding.
Inherit the bagged wind.
My spring is trying hard.
White buds flex perplexed resolve.

What dusk begins, dawn will erase.
Dear landlord. I rest my case.

End Run

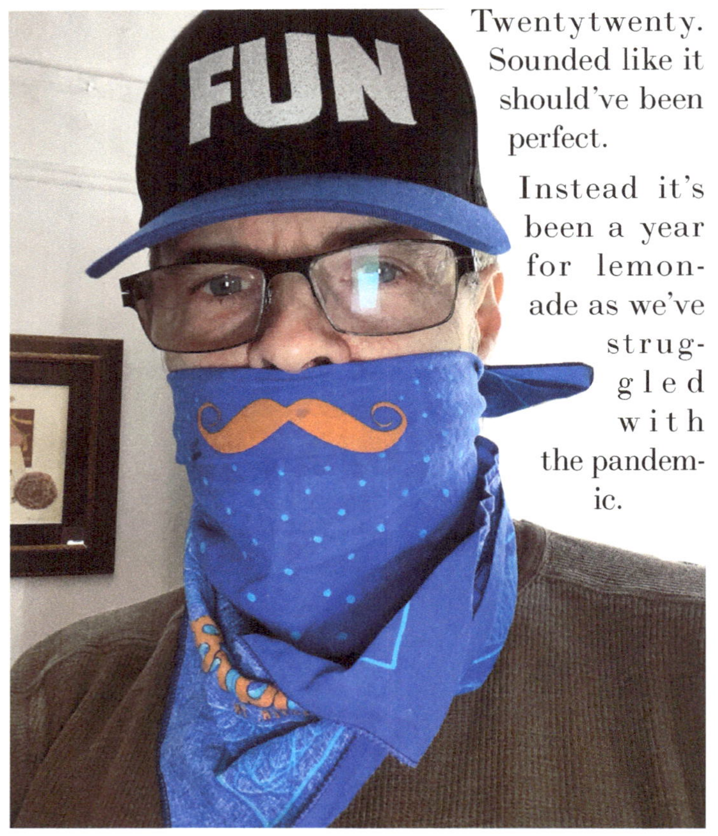

Twentytwenty. Sounded like it should've been perfect.

Instead it's been a year for lemonade as we've struggled with the pandemic.

As I write this it is December first, designated as a Day without Art, a day to honor victims of another pandemic, AIDS. Thanks **VISUAL AIDS** and all who work for others, especially our medical care givers.

It's good to have a purpose. It was a thrill to do daily FT puppet shows for my granddaughter in Chicago. Check *Pandemic Puppet Jam* on Youtube for some chuckles.

Virtual encounters are a lifeline. Thanks to **Jane Friedman** and *Howl! Happening* for continuing to find ways to share art. Jane was our first *Live Mag!* Lifetime Achievement Award winner.

Poet and publisher **Robert Hershon** accepted our second annual award at Howl! a year ago. Robert just brought out issue 111 of *Hanging Loose Magazine* (my "Madhattan Classic" included).

We continue with two awards—one to artist **Willie Birch**. Willie and I met when we were both working in the Comprehensive Employment Training Act (CETA). I've never known a more engaging artist.

We also honor writer and actor **Michael Lally**, the King of Play. Beginning in '72 with *South Orange Sonnets*, he now has over 30 books, including his most recent overview from *Seven Stories*.

Local Knowledge magazine fiction and poetry series continues on Zoom. Publisher **Sanjay Agnihotri** and I have been co-hosting readings for five years. 2020 included **Keisha-Gaye Anderson, Andrei Codrescu, David Mills, Steve Luttrell, Alan Kaufman, Sara Sarai, Bernard Meisler, Ed Sanders**, and **Luc Sante**. Bon mottist **Greg Masters** put out *Collaborations*, a redux of much of the St. Mark's 3rd gen NY School. Work by **Allen Ginsberg, Ted Berrigan, Jim Brodey, John Godfrey, Elinor Nauen, Bob Holman**, and **Nellie Vargas**; *The Disciples of Distress*, a play by Greg and me; historic photos by **Monica Clarie Antoine**, contributor **Tom Weigel**'s sister.

Thanks galleries that encourage poetry. *Lichtundfire* Director **Priska Juschka** is tireless. She's invited **Jonathan Goodman, Barry Wallenstein, Allan Coleman, Barbara Rosenthal** and more. A **Jack Youngerman** (1926-2020) painting hung the night of our book launch *(Party Everywhere)*. And *Zürcher* with **John Yau** and **Tom Devaney**.

Thanks good people at *Lit Balm*—the weekly reading series that started to keep us connected, **Jonathan Penton, Larissa Shmailo**, and **Marc Vincenz**.

Great news! Issue #18's art will be curated by **Madeline Weinrib**! Madeline and I worked together on *Cover Magazine* and she sponsored events for us at *Art In General*. Thanks Deputy Editor **Ilka Scobie** for helping set this up.

Finally, deep thanks to designer and Contributing Ed **Lori Ortiz**! Check our new online store where you can buy our back issues. Hurray to our contributors and community who have brought us through our 13th year. Best of luck to us all!

— Jeffrey Cyphers Wright

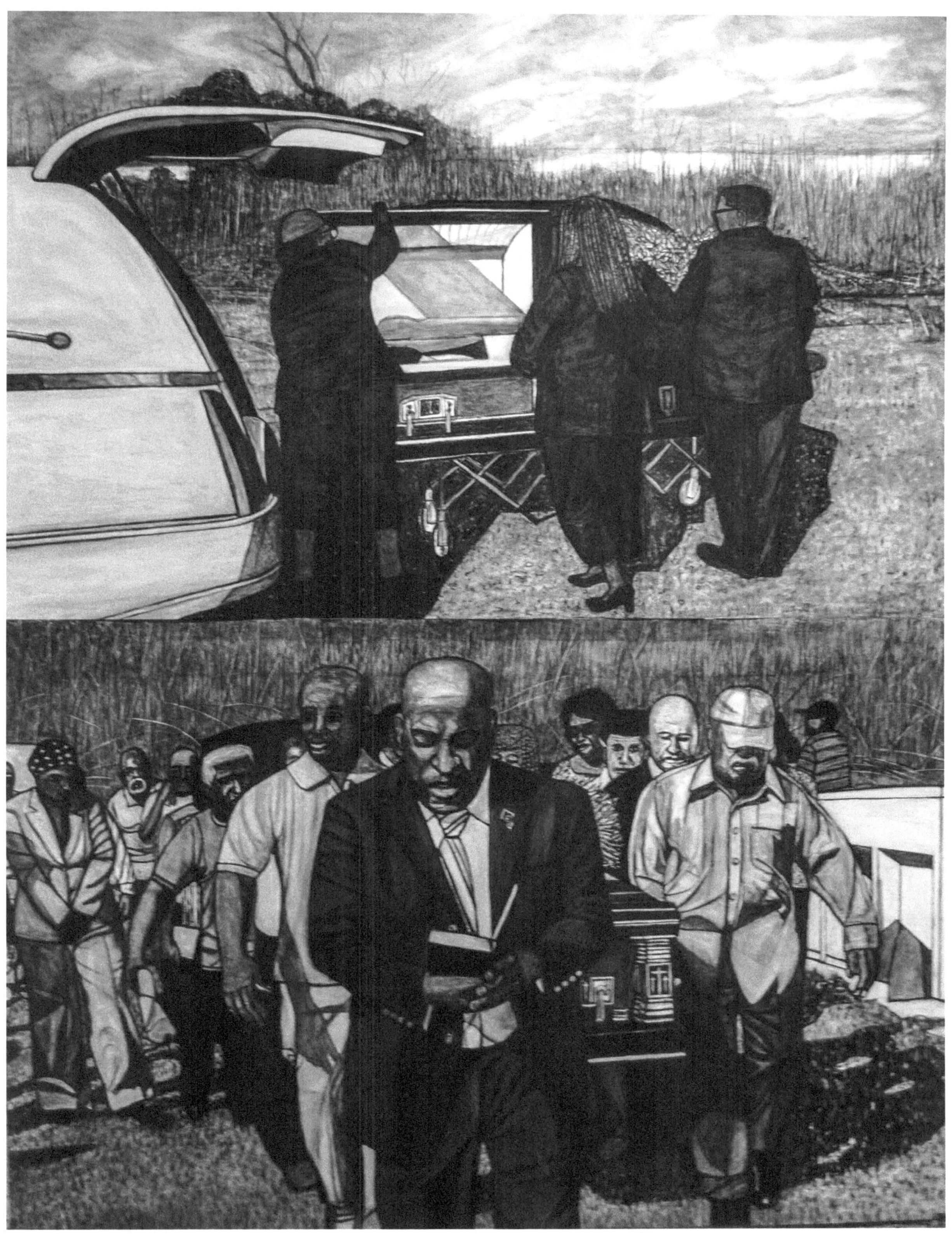

Country Funeral (Funeral for JD) 2018, charcoal and acrylic on paper diptych
Each panel 48" x 72" overall dimensions 72" x 96", courtesy @ Willie Birch

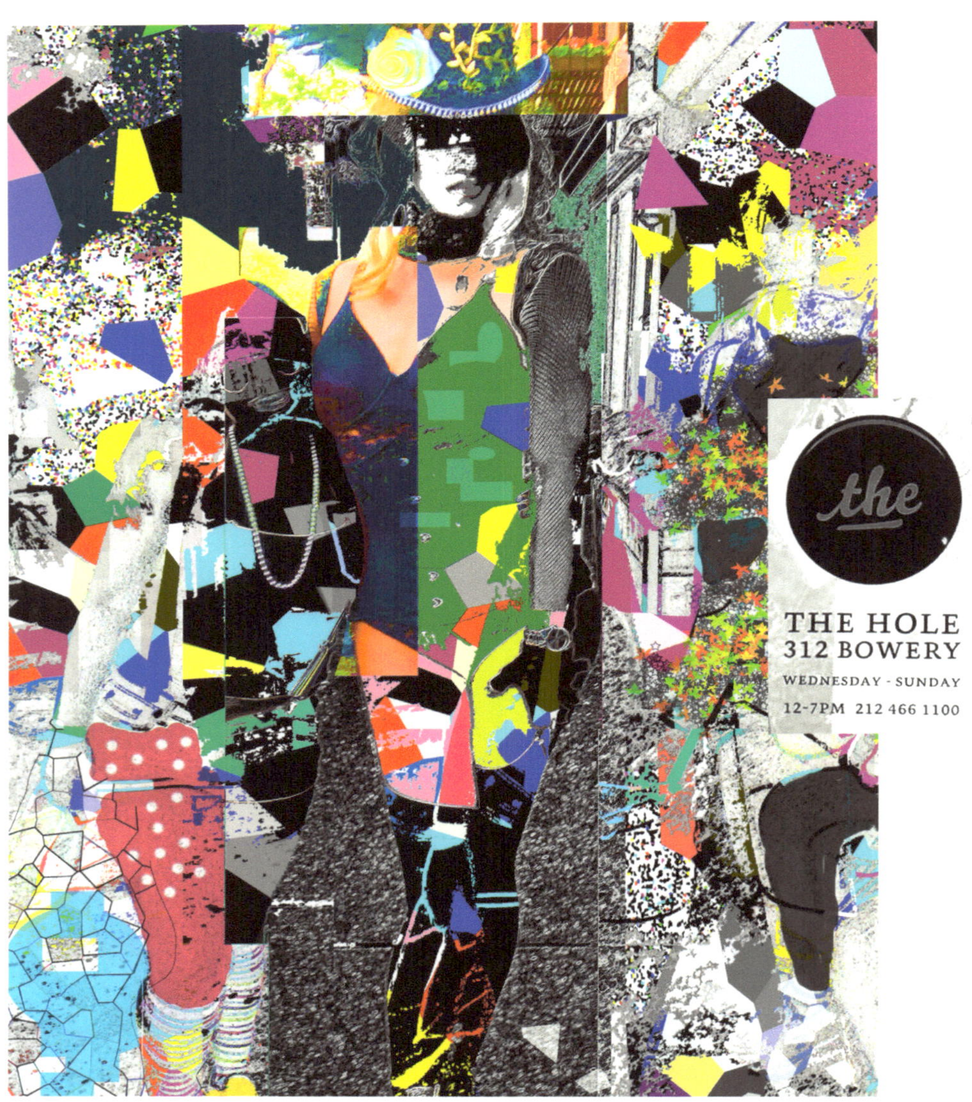

LUIGI CAZZANIGA

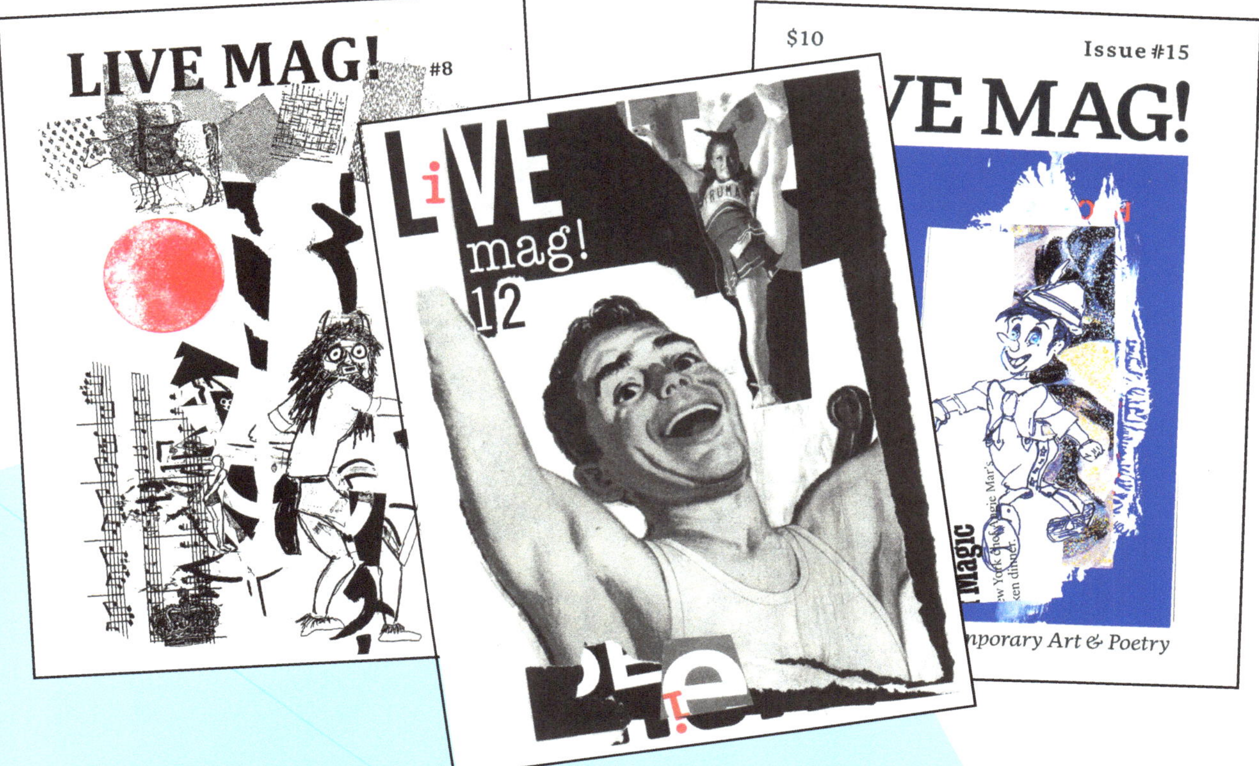

LiVE Mag!

From the stage to the page, from the wall to the journal—
each exciting issue is filled with contemporary art and poetry.
Snazzy, snappy, and savvy—order a copy of Live Mag! today!

Get your hands on a beautiful collector's item. These small editions
and rare back issues with hand-embellished covers are available.
Order directly from Live Mag! Issue 17 is also available from Ingram/
Spark.

https://store.livemag.org